Green and Profitable

BOOK 1

I0484081

# Profitable Green Business Practices

## Shel Horowitz

# Contents

# This Major Paper Company Has Been **Recycling Since 1950**

Would you believe…a household paper products company that switched to recycled raw materials in 1950, and has been producing recycled paper towels, napkins, toilet paper, and tissues ever since? A company that was so dedicated to creating "paper made from paper, not from trees"(TM) that it actually set up its own paper collection service (and currently collects paper for recycling from a 300-mile radius)? A company that saw no reason to jack up prices and has remained a consistent player in the lower price points? And a company that did this with such humility that *it didn't bother telling the public for decades,* and didn't make a big deal about it until 2009?

Yes, this company exists. Marcal, founded in 1932, went to manufacturing its paper products from recycled paper nearly 60 years ago. Small mentions had crept into the packing by the early 1990s— but only when turnaround CEO Tim Spring and several other executives were hired to bring the company back from bankruptcy in 2008 did the company realize it was sitting on a marketing goldmine. The following year, Marcal launched its Small Steps(TM) consumer brand, aimed squarely at environmentally conscious consumers. Not only is it 100% recycled, but the manufacturing process does not use chlorine bleach, the products are hypoallergenic and nearly lint-free

We could save a full million trees if every American household bought just a single roll of recycled paper towels, box of recycled tissues, or package of napkins, the company says.

What does that mean specifically? Every year, saving a million trees would:

- ✓ Keep 250 million pounds of carbon dioxide out of the air while adding 260 million pounds of oxygen (enough to supply 520 million people)

- ✓ Absorb as much carbon as is produced by a million cars each driving 26,000 miles

- ✓ Substantially reduce methane emissions (potentially a bigger problem than $CO_2$) from landfills, compared to using virgin paper

As a consumer, I became aware of recycled paper in the early 1970s, and started looking for suppliers. At that time it was very hard to find any paper identified as recycled, and even harder to find recycled paper that was high enough quality and low enough price to make the switch worth it.

In the past ten or fifteen years, it's gotten much easier. I now buy exclusively recycled paper not only for household products (where prices are comparable to standard brands) but also for my office printers (where I have to pay substantially more). When I think of how much Marcal recycled paper I would have bought in the decades starting from when I became aware until the market finally caught up, I have to wonder what took them so long.

Considering that in the few months following its introduction, Small Steps, which is in about 50 percent of US markets, has become the top-selling recycled brand, Marcal executives must be wondering the same thing. (It just proves the case I make in my eighth book Guerrilla Marketing Goes Green: Winning Strategies to Improve Your Profits and Your Planet—that it's not enough to *be* a Green company, you also have to tell the world.)

Marcal is even beginning to gather signatures on this nice little eco-pledge:

✓ I am only one person.
  But what I do impacts the whole world.

✓ I have decided that the health of the earth is important to me.
  I have decided to honor this priority in small ways.

✓ If I can share a ride or take public transportation to help save the air, I will.

✓ If I can make everyday choices that help save energy, I will.

✓ If I can choose recycled paper that help save the forests and wildlife habitats, I will.

The company is promoting the pledge through social media, appearances by its spokesperson, and through a link on its community page. I signed, and I hope you will too. Meanwhile, I've been buying Small Steps, and can report that the quality is fine.

Incidentally, in the new book, I discuss ways companies can protect themselves from accusations of greenwashing. One of those is to state honestly that you've been using recycled materials for 30 years. By 2010, Marcal was able to double that claim.

(Special thanks to Lindsay Jacob of Marcal for supplying a lot of raw material I used in researching this article.)

# Some **Big Companies** Going **Green and Profitable**

In the corporate world, if you start talking about going green, you'll often hear messages like this:

> "Yes, we're going green, despite the expense.
> It's the right thing to do."

Yes, it is the right thing to do. And yes, very small companies are often nimble enough to seize the combined economic and environmental advantages.

But smart companies of any size can go green in ways that are highly profitable. Even large, slow-moving companies can save enormously.

Want some examples?

## Southwest Airlines

Southwest expanded its on-plane and in-terminal recycling program from just aluminum cans to a much wider assortment of recycled materials. Working with a vendor who is able to handle co-mingled recyclables—which means no extra burden on flight attendants who would find it difficult to collect paper, plastic, and aluminum separately—the company is slashing a big chunk out of its multimillion dollar annual waste disposal budget.

And, as Southwest spokesperson Laurel Moffat notes, "To date, we have saved more than 37,000 trees, more than one million gallons of oil, and more than 15 million gallons of water."

For in-terminal recycling, the two airports piloting the program are diverting 12 to 19 container loads out of the waste stream every month.

## Google

The company's big, powerful servers not only hold and instantly organize much of the world's knowledge, but consume enormous quantities of electricity. Google has invested in a massive project to develop a 350-mile-long 6,000-megawatt wind-powered electrical backbone off the North Atlantic Coast of the United States— that's enough to power 1.9 million households. Stretching from Virginia to  New Jersey, these connected turbines are well-located to ease power burdens on New York, Newark, Philadelphia, Wilmington, Baltimore, and Washington.

Using the backbone model will eliminate the need to build individual transmission lines from each offshore wind project, and thus reduce the number of permits and environmental impact studies—and bring the wind plants on line much sooner.

According to Rick Needham, Google's Green Business Operations Director, the company is providing 37.5 percent of the initial-stage equity. And profit is most definitely one of Google's motives: "We believe in investing in projects that make good business sense and further the development of renewable energy. We're willing to take calculated risks on early stage ideas and projects that can have dramatic impacts while offering attractive returns," Needham says.

## The Empire State Building

New York's most famous skyscraper is shaving $4.4 million a year in energy costs—40 percent of its former $11 million annual energy bills—in a major "deep energy retrofit" that involves upgrading every single one of its 6,514 windows. For roughly $700 per window—versus $2500 each to completely replace them—each window is cleaned, coated with a thin UV-resistant film, and insulated with pressurized argon and krypton gasses. Other parts of the renovation include insulating the radiators, using both natural and artificial lighting more efficiently, wireless and portable thermostat sensors, and occupancy sensors that prevent heating or cooling of unused space. The building is also switching to individual tenant-by-tenant metering, meaning those who leave appliances and lights on when no one is using them will pay the cost of the wasted electricity.

Building manager and co-owner Anthony Malkin points out that buildings account for 80 percent of the city's energy use, and not in equal numbers. "Even more interestingly, 20 percent of the buildings consume 80 percent of that energy. So 64 percent of all energy consumed in New York City is consumed by 20 percent of the buildings. That really took me by surprise."

This project could easily be replicated elsewhere, because the impact on profitability is huge. Look at the numbers: The project cost is $13.2 million, and the annual return (savings) is $4.4 million. That means the first 3 years pay for the project (that's an ROI of 33% a year). And the second three years put an extra $13.2 million into profit! With banks paying a measly 1.07 percent on a one-year and 2.3 percent return even on a 5-year CD right now, a 33 percent return is mighty attractive.

How much oil and coal could we eliminate, and how much capital would be freed up for job creation, if every company took just one of its buildings through a deep-energy retrofit process?

# Going Green: Private Sector Must Take Up the Slack

Many observers in the environmental movement were dispirited by the US election results in November [2010], with the election of several prominent climate-change deniers and the power switch in the House of Representatives.

Political reality around sustainability varies a lot with location. Western Europe has been pushing hard on green technology leadership for years, combining business and government to drive the change. From simple innovations like a light/heavy switch for toilet flushes  to the complexities of generating significant power from offshore and mountaintop wind farms, Europe has made it clear that carbon reduction and energy and water conservation are priorities. China, using an approach dictated largely by government policy, has become a world leader in solar.

However, both the European and Chinese systems send out mixed messages. Europe relies far too heavily on dangerous and un-green nuclear power; China has made an even larger commitment to dirty, health-killing coal.

In many parts of Africa and Asia, NGOs and nonprofits—often more than government or private industry—are taking the lead, bringing low-cost and highly portable energy technologies in to disadvantaged villages, replacing polluting, unsafe, and carbon-spewing kerosene, wood, and charcoal with clean alternatives—decentralized to the level of a single home.

Turning back to the US: I believe the election shows that Americans can't rely on the federal government to deal with climate change on our behalf; as business leaders and thought leaders, we have to do it ourselves. Nothing meaningful will come out of Washington for the next two gridlocked years, on climate change, going green, or many other issues.

But this doesn't mean the work will stop. Not at all.

Individuals within companies will continue to spearhead the movement for change, and those companies will slowly turn to embrace the change. Individuals within households will continue to make better choices for themselves and their families, and the machinery of commerce will continue to make those choices ever more widely available and affordable.

First, of course, is the pioneering work done for the past several decades by companies that were founded with a strong environmental chromosome. When companies like Whole Foods or Ben & Jerry's take steps to go more green, it's totally in keeping with the corporate culture—the company DNA—and with the needs and desires of their customer base.

But wider change must be driven by companies considered much more mainstream. "Fringe" businesses—small innovative concerns that will grow to become the Whole Foods and Ben & Jerry's of the future—may show us how to get there, but to really make a difference, much bigger players have to get involved.

Will this happen without government carrots? Actually, it's happening already. Let's take Walmart as an example. The largest retailer in the world—that sounds pretty mainstream. Founded by a conservative, pickup-driving rural American from the South (the most conservative region in the country), Walmart certainly doesn't kowtow to tree-huggers. In fact, it's often been criticized by environmentalists for a host of issues ranging from store siting to labor practices.

Yet in the last few years, starting with the appointment of Lee Scott as CEO and continuing past his term, Walmart has taken numerous major steps toward sustainability in both its operations and its product line. Why?

1. Walmart's always been awesome at slashing the cost and boosting the efficiency of its logistics. So the dozens of green operations initiatives that actually save the company millions of dollars are a no-brainer. Examples range from fitting its long-haul trucks with separate temperature systems so the big diesels don't have to run just to heat or cool the cab, to switching to LED parking lot lighting in some stores—which slashed energy consumption by 48 percent and maintenance costs by 75 percent—to saving 678,000 barrels of oil and 290,000 metric tons of greenhouse gases a year just by cutting plastic shopping bag waste by a third.

2. The company realized that bringing in green product lines (from energy-efficient light bulbs to organic food to

healthy cleaning and body care lines) opened up enormous revenue and profit potential.

In other words, the company realized it could both save a fortune and make a fortune. So what's not to like? And this is the future of going green in the US for the next two years: companies stepping forward to do the right thing out of economic self-interest.

Of course, if the Obama administration had engaged in a massive Marshall Plan-style program to create hundreds of thousands of jobs by converting to green power sources, we might not need to ask ourselves how to move forward without the government's help. But that's a topic for a different column.

# Sustainability Innovators
## Around the World

Every once in a while, I'll devote this column to a roundup of some of the coolest sustainability initiatives I've come across anywhere in the world. This is the first installment, featuring five different ventures on five different continents, and business models that include an architect working solo, a manufacturing corporation, a nonprofit, and a couple of small companies.

### United States
### Kenguru—Sustainable Independence for Wheelchair Users

Think about how many resources are consumed by a standard wheelchair van. A huge vehicle with complicated, slow, hydraulic lifts: expensive in both money and materials to build, and consuming huge amounts of fuel to operate.

Now...reinvent the whole thing: a one-person electric vehicle, tiny, secure, and empowering the wheelchair user to control his or her own transportation. The user rolls in up a ramp through a rear hatch facing the curb, fastens the chair, and then it's off to work, play, or whatever.
www.kenguru.com

## Australia
### Freemantle Timber Traders—Turning Old Buildings Into New Building Materials

This company has designed its own tools to salvage lumber from demolition projects in ways it claims provides much cleaner, more intact hardwood lumber than conventional demolition and salvage techniques. If the greenest building is the one that's already been built, the next-greenest might be the one that uses materials from buildings that existed and were taken down. www.fremantletimbertraders.com.au/profile.asp, community page at www.facebook.com/environmentaltimber.


## Hong Kong
### Gary Chang Maximizes Every Inch of 344-square foot Apartment

This may be the tiniest apartment in the world to have full kitchen and bath, a well-equipped bar, guest quarters, and 24 rooms (though not all at the same time). Using movable walls, foldable surfaces, and other tricks, this ingenious architect shows that it's possible to live quite luxuriously in a very small space. At one time, there were seven people living there! Buckminster Fuller would be proud. Video tour (two minutes):

blogs.wsj.com/developments/2010/04/28/hong-kong-architect-crams-24-rooms-into-344-square-feet/

## Evocative Design—Who Needs Styrofoam Peanuts When You've Got Mushrooms?

It's hard to imagine too many products less environmentally friendly than Styrofoam. Even experienced plastics recyclers usually can't figure out what to do it. And, in my personal opinion, it ruins the taste of food or hot drinks stored in it.

A whole lot of Styrofoam gets turned into packing peanuts. And even if you have good intentions and take them down to your local shipping store to reuse, some of them always get away and get stepped on, wedged into things, or become a nuisance in other ways.

So why not avoid the problem in the first place and find a natural, compostable packing material? Evocative Design offers packing made from cottonseed and buckwheat hulls, held together with filaments made from mushroom roots—while saving 85 percent of the energy and reducing 90 percent of the carbon dioxide compared with Styrofoam.

planetforward.ca/blog/packing-peanuts-meet-a-replacement-that-is-grown-from-mushrooms/

## Burkina Faso (and three other African countries): Association la Voute Nubienne Creates Timberless Housing

Deforestation is a huge problem in sub-Saharan Africa, and the loss of forest often leads to desertification—exacerbating hunger and other social ills in the process. Cross-pollinating a vaulted-roof housing construction technique from the Nubian culture in Egypt (on the other side of the continent) with local labor and non-wood earth bricks made from local materials, a French nonprofit has been building sustainable homes and community buildings, and creating jobs. The houses cost only about $100 each to build, and make a real difference

in these economically marginal communities. There is a bit of plastic sheeting involved in waterproofing the roof, but the house can be built without sheet metal and without timber supports, unlike the usual building styles in the Sahel region.

An English-language page about the construction technique is at www.lavoutenubienne.org/-The-VN-Technical-Solution; if you'd like to donate, the group is set up with Global Giving at www.globalgiving.org/projects/help-build-sustainable-africa-houses/people/.

# Easy **Money-Saving** **Green Tips** for Business

Environmental measures can be easy or hard. Go for the easy stuff with the biggest return first. For example:

Most businesses leak huge quantities of heated air in the winter and cooled air in the summer. Simple and very inexpensive measures like insulating outlets and switchplates with foam gaskets (and plugging unused outside-wall outlets with baby outlet protectors) on outside-facing walls can make an immediate difference. So can making sure windows are properly caulked. And ensuring that doors to the outside close tightly and have weatherstripping and heat-trapping rubber sweeps.

Install programmable thermostats to stop heating/cooling air when the building is shut for the night—and program them properly: no more than 68° F/ 20° C in the winter, no lower than 75° F/24° C in the summer during working hours, and perhaps 55° F/13° C in the winter and 85° F/29° C in the summer, from half an hour after the end of the workday until half an hour before employees start arriving in the morning.

Plug computers, machinery, and appliances into smart power strips that eliminate "energy vampires" by cutting power to the device when it's not in use—and train your people to flip the power strips off if they're the last to leave at night.

Cut your paper costs by 40 percent or so by switching to duplexing (two-sided) printers and copiers, setting them to default to two-sided, and training your employees to use that setting when possible. Have a goal that the only single-sided copies are the last pages of documents with an odd number of pages. The amount of paper that can be saved will shock you.

Of course, some few documents do need to be printed one-sided. But often, that's because they're going to be used as a reprint master—which can be avoided by printing from a digital file instead of a hard copy, gaining higher quality in the process.

Encourage employees to do more on screen and print less in the first place. Demonstrate the computer settings that display larger print without changing the actual document (for instance, the View-Zoom feature in Microsoft Word and most Internet browsing software)—this makes reading on the screen a lot more comfortable, and printing a lot less necessary.

Recycle all the scrap paper in your office. Recycle plastic and metal as well. And switch to recycled copy paper, toilet paper, and paper towels; these days, the latter two don't have to cost any more than non-recycled, and copy paper is only a bit more.

Change your break room and lounges around with a goal of sustainability: Get rid of disposable cups and buy each employee a personalized coffee mug, plus a few for visitors. Use reusable rags and sponges instead of paper towels. Switch to organic fair-trade coffee, tea, and cocoa. If your business is in a place where the water is drinkable, add a water filter to the sink and educate your employees that using filtered tap water is much greener than bottled, as well as much cheaper for them.

Partner with a local organic farm to offer a once-a-week farmers market in your parking lot or on a lawn, where employees can stock up on fresh organic veggies—this costs you nothing, and your people will love it (especially if they live in cities).

Switch to natural/organic pest control and landscaping.

Install an aerator on every faucet.

Prohibit smoking on your campus—but first, announce the deadline,  and in the meantime, provide smoking-cessation assistance for employees who need it. (You'll pay for the program through savings in reduced absesm for health reasons, and possibly lower insurance costs. You may also be able to get grant funding or tap into no-cost quit-smoking programs.)

Next, look at steps you can take to make your employees more comfortable and happier, which in turn will make them more productive. Bring houseplants into work areas—they chew up carbon dioxide (a major greenhouse gas) and turn it into oxygen. Provide natural lighting where possible. Use fresh air from open windows during the spring and fall, if your building is set up with windows that open. Use curtains and drapes to let in sun in the winter, block it out during the hot summer—and to keep heat in during winter nights, while releasing it in summer.

These, of course, are only the tip of the iceberg. We can all cut energy, water, and waste in thousands of ways, many of which, like the measures above, cost little or nothing.

Set aside the money you save from these measures to look at more complex steps, such as adding more insulation, auditing your manufacturing process for energy savings, switching to low-water or even waterless toilets, planting an area of your roof or adding solar panels, going through the LEED or EnergyStar certification process, and so on.

And don't forget to start talking about all the green things you're doing in your marketing, on your website, and in your press releases. The marketing benefit alone in some cases, can be enough to cover the capital cost of the next round of improvements.

# A **Whole Country** that Runs on **Renewable Energy**

I've known for years that Iceland is a geothermal paradise, so when we went there this summer, I made sure to pay some attention to the power supply.

As it turned out, that was absurdly easy to do. You can't travel in Iceland without encountering the power of geothermal energy, and many Icelanders we met bragged about their geothermal systems. We even encountered several museum exhibits highlighting volcanic and geothermal activity.

 We visited a geothermal power plant that contained an energy museum. We cooked eggs in a geothermal spring, and tasted bread that had been baked in the ground, overnight.

While there is significant use of hydropower along with geothermal, we saw almost no solar in Iceland—in part because usually they don't have too much sun, and in part because geothermal and hydro readily available and produce much steadier (and cheaper) power.

In the United States, where I live, harnessing geothermal typically involves drilling below the earth to a layer with year-round consistent temperature at about 50°F/10°C, and tapping into that layer to boost heating in the winter, and cooling in the summer. I live in the northeast United States, in a region called New England, where temperatures typically range from -5°F/-20.5°C on a cold winter night to around 95°F/35°C on a sunny, hot summer afternoon. And in fact, my neighbors just put in a geothermal system, in their house built in 1747. Like most geothermal installations in the US, they are using the thermal power directly, to heat and cool water.

In actively volcanic Iceland, it's a different story. Temperatures in many of the hot springs are hot enough to kill a person quickly, approaching the boiling point of water (212°F/100°C).

All you have to do is feel the temperature of the water coming out of the hot tap to know that geothermal means something different in Iceland. It's HOT! As hot as the solar-heated water I use in my home, which is to say hotter than any  tap water I've encountered from fossil-heated sources. Our water is so hot that we warn our guests about how not to scald themselves in the shower. So that aspect of Iceland felt very familiar.

There are several differences, though:

First, the water at home smells of the chlorine that municipal authorities use to purify it. In many parts of Iceland, including the capital, Reykjavík, the water smells strongly of sulfur—so strongly that my toothbrush would smell like elderly eggs, hours after brushing.

Another difference is the ubiquity of the system. Geothermal is heavily commercialized in Iceland. Municipalities harness and pipe it into virtually every house and building, as well as the numerous geothermally heated municipal swimming pools and hot tubs (up to 111°F/44°C) that were in literally every town we visited—one of the few bargains in a rather expensive country, where practically everything else has to be imported. But in the

US, geothermal systems are purchased by the individual homeowner, and are expensive enough that people are very cautious about making such a large investment. My neighbors spent $38,000 on their system.

And fourth, I was surprised at how much geothermal power is used to create steam and spin turbines to generate electricity, and how much of that electricity is transported across significant distances; I'd expected most of it to be heating water for direct use rather than spinning turbines, and to be used near the point of origin, as it is at home. Transporting energy across distances cuts down on efficiency.

But efficiency and conservation aren't such big concerns in Iceland. We were rather surprised that saving water or electricity didn't seem to be a value. People just ran the water or left lights on. Their attitude was that they had plenty, it was really cheap, and they didn't have to worry about running out.

Personally, I think that's shortsighted. They may have plenty now, but that could change in the future, especially as the country begins exporting to parts of Europe that are not so richly endowed with power. I think the conservation-isn't-important attitude will change with education and a values shift, just as it has shifted in Asia, North America, and especially continental Europe. Meanwhile, Iceland can truly claim to have one of the greenest power grids in the world.

In a country with only 318,452 inhabitants and approximately 116,000 households as of January 2011, this tiny country has the capacity to supply much of Europe's energy needs. In fact, plans are afoot to build deep-sea cables that will export as much as 5 billion kilowatt-hours of clean, renewable electricity to the rest of Europe—enough to power 1.25 million homes. Those of you based in Europe, especially, should be on the lookout for opportunities to profit from this coming industrial shift. And those in other seismically active parts of the world might want to think about how to get your country into massive geothermal.

# As Green Gets More **Complex**... It Also Gets **Easier**

As a long-term marketer, media-watcher and journalist, I learned long ago that you can tell a whole lot about market trends, as well as the thinking and feeling patterns of not just the overall culture but also the cultures of subgroups within niches—just by studying the ads aimed at them. And you can find out a great deal about people's hot buttons and how to persuade.

When large corporations pay good money to display an ad, it means their research shows their customers want to buy the sorts of products, services, or ideas described in those ads, and that at least a percentage of them will respond to the types of language, graphics, and offers that those ads encompass.

Here's an example directly related to the green world:

I'm looking at a magazine published by McGraw-Hill, about as mainstream a publisher as you can find. The magazine, called GreenSource: The Magazine of Sustainable Design, is aimed at green architects, designers, and builders.

Firstly, it says a great deal that the green design and construction niche is big enough to get attention from a publisher like McGraw-Hill, and that this magazine seems to have no trouble finding advertisers, even in a down economy.

And secondly, by looking at the ads, I'm reminded that the bar has gone sharply higher for sustainable design over the past few years. Going green, and being able to convince a skeptical green consumer base that you've done so, is a lot deeper now than simply using recycled materials, driving a hybrid, or caulking all the drafty spaces. All sorts of new issues are coming into play. Layers of complexity I never would have dreamed would become mainstream factors are now being talked about every day.

Here are just the ads in the first eight pages (before the Table of Contents):

The first is a two-page ad is for recycled ceiling panels. And joining the trend toward making claims believable by quantifying them, the ad claims 100 million pounds of old ceiling tiles were reclaimed, keeping 50,000 tons of them out of landfills. These two numbers happen to be equivalent—perhaps the copywriter wasn't sure which would have greater impact, and so used both.

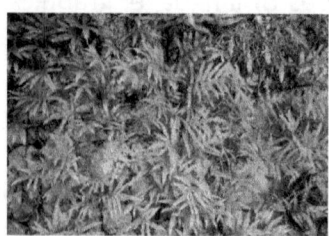

Turning the page—another two-page ad, for a "living wall": "biofilter technology [that] not only captures airborne pollutants, it breaks them down." The pictures show a standing forest on the left, a multistory building wall covered with plants on the right.

The outer half of the next page has a half-page vertical ad for "vertical landscaping" (appropriately enough). It shows plants growing thickly on the outside of a two-story townhouse. The inner half of the page is the magazine's masthead. Opposite, a full-page ad for "the only gypsum board that clears the air." This one claims to permanently remove Volatile Organic Compounds (VOCs) for up to 75 years.

On the next page, another half-page vertical for "drivable grass®"—a driveway paving replacement that allows storm water to drain through to the soil underneath. And opposite that, a full-page ad for a low-emissions certification agency.

The last ad before the contents page is for an aluminum building material with 70- to 80 percent post-consumer recycled content, and ISO certification to prove it.

Walls that filter rather than emit pollutants, and paving solutions that recycle the rainwater—were these the kinds of things you expected to be dealing with when you decided to take your company green? I didn't think so. It all sounds so complicated!

But consider the positive side: if this level of awareness is becoming so common that these are the advertisers in the prized (and expensive) front-of-the-book pages at a major-publisher magazine, *that creates a huge opening for you to push for greater sustainability measures in your company.* You can use this kind of magazine to prove to the powers-that-be that the world isn't standing still, and that your organization needs to both be doing more on sustainability, and finding ways to convey that commitment to the public.

And that may turn out to be a very exciting task.

# What's the **Right Clean Energy Solution** for You?

So, you've made the decision to convert all or part of your energy use to clean, renewable sources? Congratulations on a great decision— but now how do you decide among all these alternatives: various forms of solar, wind, hydro, geothermal, as well as more exotic formats like magnetic and tidal? The choice may seem bewildering.

These two principles may help you figure it out. First, do conservation first, and second, pick the best alternative based on conditions on-site.

## Conservation First

Energy you save outright is energy you don't need to generate or harvest. As one very prominent example, New York City's iconic Empire State Building enlisted the Rocky Mountain Institute and other groups to design and implement a "deep energy retrofit" that's saving over $4 million every year. While the $13 million investment was not cheap, the 33% annual ROI far outpaces any conventional investment vehicle and will continue to pay multimillion dollar dividends for decades.

Not every business has the capital for that kind of program. But the good news is every business can find ways to save at least a few percentage points on up to as much as 80 percent of energy consumption. Whether the investment is small or large, the payback can be quick (and the savings reinvested in more energy conservation). If you only need half as much power as you did before, you can put in a smaller and cheaper alternative energy system.

Conservation can be as simple as turning off unneeded lights and computers or as complex as completely redesigning and rebuilding an industrial process. Do an energy audit with a consultant who can see not just the usual incremental measures but also the potential for sweeping, big-picture changes. For the Empire State Building, that actually meant temporarily converting a floor of the building into a factory to convert the old windows into highly efficient ones, on-site (among other improvements).

## Find the Right Alternative

Once you've reduced your energy footprint through conservation, it's time to research your alternative energy options. When possible, generate the power you need as close to the point of use as you can. Enormous quantities of energy get wasted in transmission and transportation of energy, so it will almost always be better to produce on-site. Thus, a rooftop solar array or ground-level wind turbine makes more sense in most cases than piping in electricity from a photovoltaic farm hundreds of kilometers away.

Each energy system is going to be better suited to some installations than others. Factoring in any grants and tax incentives, how many years can you expect for payback, and thus what is your ROI?

Without in any way trying to substitute for a professional evaluation, here at least are some quick guidelines:

## Solar

Is it sunny more often than cloudy? Do you have adequate exposure: an area that gets good sun and is not in the shadow of a tall building, a mountain, or a tree canopy? If looking at rooftops, will your roof support the added weight of solar infrastructure? If

looking at ground installation, can you install the system so as to permit other uses (for example, an employee community garden) underneath? Do you have a vehicle fleet that could be converted to solar and used to recharge the grid? Do you have room and budget for both solar thermal (e.g., hot water) and photovoltaic (electricity generation), and if not, which should you do first?

## Wind

Does your location have steady but relatively modest wind—fast enough to spin the blades, but not so fast that it tears the system apart in a year or two? Will your neighbors put up a big fight that makes the project too expensive and uncomfortable? Have you looked into less intrusive systems such as low-to-the-ground vertical-axis turbines?

## Hydro

Are you sited near a river or stream? Can you use technology that captures energy from the moving water directly, or will you need to build a dam? If you're damming a body of water, have you fully analyzed the environmental impact? Can you use the water to directly run a mill, or will you be using it to generate electricity?

## Geothermal

Do you have enough land to put in a system? Can you harness that energy for enough uses (space heating and cooling, water heating) to justify the substantial capital cost? Do you live in Iceland, where your energy is already geothermal?

## Contributing to the Solution

Whichever technology turns out to be right for your location, moving toward clean renewables is a great move. Installing a system that's right for your site will lower your energy costs and carbon footprint, while contributing at least a little bit toward preventing catastrophic climate change. So do your part—but "do it smart."

# One **Product**, Multiple **Benefits**

Do more with less—makes sense when you're thinking green, doesn't it—especially when you let it expand your idea of what's possible.

A guiding principle in thinking green is to achieve multiple purposes with a single item. The item could be a product, a component, a service, or maybe even an idea. Systems that incorporate this principle are generally much more sustainable, need fewer components, and are therefore also more economical.

Does that sound like a bunch of abstractions that's a bit too complicated to puzzle out? Let's look at some specific examples.

## Purus Pavers: Old Soda Bottles Solve Water Runoff Problems

Green builders are discovering eco-friendly substitutes for the traditional asphalt paving area. Asphalt prevents water from seeping into the ground and diverts it—usually into sewers, but sometimes into places where it causes harmful erosion.

By contrast, a paving system that allows the water to drain back into the ground right there and yet insulates vehicles from the problems of parking or driving directly on the ground can maintain the water table, reduce concentrations of toxic contaminants, eliminate the erosion problem, and even allow for plantings that grow close to the ground—

thus adding oxygen and reducing CO2 emissions, which in turn help preserve the earth in the face of catastrophic climate change.

These pavers create a latticework of support above an open area, so the water can freely drain, right where the rain falls.

I've seen concrete pavers like this, and they're very cool. A company called Purus <www.purus-plastics.de/en/ecorasterr/ecorasterr-s50.html> decided to take things up a notch, and make the pavers out of recycled polyethylene from old soda bottles. This adds several more benefits: longer lasting landfills, avoiding toxic fumes from incineration of plastic (which should NEVER be burned), reuse of materials, among others.

## Ocean Arks International: Waste Becomes Raw Material in a Closed Loop

Instead of the typical open system where an industrial process creates waste that is released into the environment, enviro-pioneer John Todd keeps asking how we can close the loop by using that waste as an input for something else.

After all, that's what happens in nature: humans and other animals breathe in oxygen and breathe out carbon dioxide, while plants breathe in that carbon dioxide and breathe oxygen back out. A dead tree becomes habitat for nesting birds, and when the birds die, their nutrients are absorbed back into the soil where plants can use them.

The company Todd founded, Ocean Arks International, takes this single simple idea in amazing directions. For instance, an integrated system of businesses and activities called The Intervale <www.intervale.org/>, in Burlington, Vermont, uses brewery waste to grow mushrooms, mushroom waste to feed fish, fish waste to grow hydroponic vegetables, and so on

Expanding the principle again, Todd and his colleagues design and build restorative ecosystems that reduce carbon, digest human-caused waste, and revivify dead or dying bodies of water. (Click here to read more about John Todd's work)

## Organic and Biodynamic Farming: Benefiting All Stakeholders

The last example is one that most of us are familiar with: organic farming, and its more tightly regulated cousin, Demeter Certified Biodynamic agriculture <www.demeterbta.com/>.

You already know that organic foods not only eliminate harmful chemicals but also typically produce tastier foods. But you might not know that organic agriculture can sequester 7000 pounds of carbon per acre...that agriculture can raise a significant portion of our energy needs through oilseed crops like sunflowers (yes, I'm aware there are issues in using cropland for energy)...that a good organic diet of grasses and flax can significantly reduce the (very troubling greenhouse gas) methane emissions from cow burps...and that a cow fed an organic diet will be far more profitable for farmers, because she is likely to live up to three times as long, have many more lactation cycles, and even yield 20 percent more beef. (These statistics are taken from my report on the 2011 Sustainable Foods Summit held in San Francisco: <greenandprofitable.com/its-about-tradeoffs-part-1/>).

## And You?

These are just three of thousands of examples. How can you incorporate holistic, systemic thinking to create multiple benefits with one innovation?

# Green as **Sexy**

As a good follow-up to last month's column on marketing green products to nongreen audience, let's take things a notch higher.

As you read this, I'm off to Houston, Texas, USA, to give a speech called "Making Green Sexy" at a green buildings conference.

The interesting thing about that idea is that "sexy" is in the eye of the beholder—which is a good thing for those of us who don't look like supermodels and still manage to have loving relationships.

Last month, I mentioned the Tesla roadster, something that would fit most people's definition of sexy. It's a super-sporty car, full of Coke-bottle curves. It screams speed, power, luxury, and high status. (If you don't know what it looks like, you can see pictures at http://www.teslamotors.com/roadster). It also happens to be the most high-performance electric car that's ever been out on the market.

Yes, I'll be showing a picture of the Tesla roadster in my talk in Texas. But I'll also show a picture of Amory Lovins' ultra-efficient house (built back in 1983 in the Colorado Rockies), which is not what most people would define as sexy—at least until they look closely.

What makes Lovins' home sexy is not its looks—which are unusual, and certainly not in keeping with today's styles (though certainly reasonably attractive to my eyes). Rather, this is what I find sexy about it:

- ✓ Despite the cold, snowy winters and hot, sunny summers in the Aspen, Colorado snowbelt (one of the downhill skiing capitals of the United States), this house has neither a furnace nor an air conditioner—because it doesn't need either one.

- ✓ The sunroom is warm enough, even during the winter, that Lovins actually grows bananas inside.

- ✓ At 4000 square feet/371.6 square meters, it's big enough to compare with the grand mansions that we popularly think of as sexy.

- ✓ Because expensive items like heating and cooling systems weren't purchased, the extra-cost green and sustainable energy features paid for themselves in just 10 months.

- ✓ As a passive solar home, much of the energy savings was achieved by thinking, designing, and building holistically, where a single component might achieve multiple goals; he referred to one arch in his house that accomplishes 12 different functions.

- ✓ Long before the term "cradle-to-cradle" came into use, this house was designed to close as many loops as possible, and to produce almost no waste.

- ✓ Even using 1983 technology, which we in the solar and green world would consider quite primitive by today's standards, the house makes nearly all of its own electricity (when I heard Lovins speak several years ago, he said he averaged a USD $5 electric bill for the residential portion of his home/office—and even if higher energy prices have brought that up to, say, $25, that's still quite remarkable).

What's really sexy to me about the Lovins house is not even the individual features. It's the potential for world-wide planet-saving. Think about what kind of world we'd be living in right now if for the past 29 years since Lovins proved it was feasible, most houses had been built along these lines.

- ✓ Atmospheric carbon would be greatly reduced—probably well below the 350 parts-per-million danger zone that we are now exceeding—and thus, global warming would not be a desperate situation.

- ✓ Pollution from burning fossil fuels (and from extracting them from the earth) would be a tiny fraction of what it is now, and this in turn would mean sharply reduced healthcare costs—because a lot fewer people would be getting sick.

- ✓ Because there would be no need for the world's largest economies to chase after oil reserves, foreign policy would have been reshaped—away from wars over energy resources and toward inspiring real democracy and economic self-sufficiency

- ✓ And finally, all that capital that's been spent on buying energy would have been freed up to invest elsewhere causing a flowering of technology and the arts, and a massive rise in living standards around the world.

This kind of world should have been our inheritance. Let's at least make it our legacy.

# Simple and Elegant Solutions to Complex Environmental Problems

If your goal is to let astronauts write in deep space, you could spend millions of dollars researching, designing, and prototyping pens that will work without gravity—or you could simply hand out a box of pencils. Maybe they could even be special pencils that make a deeper, darker writing imprint and don't fade quickly (such pencils already exist).

Just as in the space program, in the world of complex environmental problems, the best solution is often surprisingly simple and very elegant. And we as green business people need to find those solutions, bring them to consumers—and market their benefits.

The massive consumer products company Procter & Gamble understands this concept and has capitalized on it. Company engineers realized that one of the biggest consumers of energy in households is heating water, and one of the largest uses of hot water is laundry. You could attack that problem with complex solutions such as heating the water with solar systems—or you could market a detergent that works perfectly well in cold water.

P&G chose the latter course, and developed Tide Coldwater, which it actively markets both as a green product to the green market, and as a money-saving product for the general consumer market. If you visit www.tidecoldwater.com on a Flash-enabled computer, the first thing you get is a calculator that allows US residents to figure out exactly how much they'd save by washing in cold water, state by state, according to their own laundry habits.

Of course, you don't really need Tide Coldwater for these savings. I find that my clothes come out just fine in cold water, using a store brand high-efficiency liquid detergent. But P&G's marketing for this brand has focused heavily on the green benefits, and they are reaching a lot of people who had been using hot water to wash.

However, the big lesson here is the simple and elegant solution. For the average householder, it's going to be far cheaper to reduce water heating energy by 30 percent or so than to install a greener hot water system. For tenants who would never pony up a big capital investment to improve a property they don't own, cold-water washing is an extremely sensible choice.

In my latest book, Guerrilla Marketing Goes Green, I discuss in some detail the work of two practical visionaries who are really good at solving complex problems with simple elegance: John Todd and Amory Lovins.

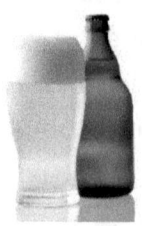

Decades before most people had ever heard of concepts like "zero waste" and "cradle-to-cradle," Todd grasped the simple and elegant concept that the waste from one production process could almost always be raw material for another one. And you can create an ecosystem of several of these processes layered together.

Thus, spent grain at a brewery turns out to be a perfect growing medium for commercial mushroom production, and that in turn generates a very nice fish food. He has used this single insight to develop biological systems that actually clean and restore polluted wetlands, rivers, and lakes. Another of his innovations in water purification is a simple tube running through the desert that uses the natural range of temperature conditions to sterilize safe drinking water in a refugee camp, no chemicals needed.

For Lovins, the three simple and elegant ideas are:

1) You can design for such deep conservation that you don't need to buy big expensive systems like furnaces and air conditioners—and the savings on these capital costs, along with the savings on energy, pay for the improvements. He has designed homes that didn't need heating or air conditioning in climates ranging from the deep-winter Colorado Rocky Mountains (where his own 1983 home is a showplace for what's possible) to places where temperatures exceeding 100°F/40°C are common.

2) Enormous amounts of energy is wasted in transmission losses. If you generate power where you need it, you need considerably less than if you transport it across great distances.

3) One design component can achieve multiple purposes.

Here are a few more examples of simple elegance addressing other environmental issues:

- ✓ Pole-mounted solar collectors allow the ground underneath them to be used for agriculture

- ✓ Bicycles, bike trailers, pedicabs, and all the other variations on pedal-powered transport of people and goods

- ✓ Small-space "vertical gardens" let apartment-dwellers grow their own food in about one square meter/square yard

- ✓ The simple mesh nets we use to keep birds from devouring our berry crops—no pesticides needed or wanted

**Simple innovations like these create huge market opportunities for pioneering green entrepreneurs.**

# Green Variations on Traditional Business

As the world gets smarter about the need to go green, millions of consumers are looking for greener ways of doing the things they've been doing all along. And smart businesses owners are right there with them, offering greener ways to do business and spreading their green attitude.

Here are a few among numerous examples of businesses that are successfully filling that green market niche.

## Green Real Estate

More and more brokers are actively marketing green properties. A few have gone so far as to affiliate themselves with green real estate broker associations such as EcoBroker.com. The home page of EcoBroker triages visitors into three  channels: consumers who want to buy or sell a green home; brokers who'd like to get certified as green-aware; and vendors of green products and services who could benefit from an affiliate relationship—everything from green architects and builders to suppliers of renewable energy certificates.

(This section uses a fairly expensive paid-placement model, and as of this writing, most of the categories are empty—rather surprising for a website launched in 2004, and disconcerting for visitors. If I were EcoBroker, I'd either switch to free basic listings with payment for enhanced, or get rid of any categories that have no entries.)

Where the site does build trust is in the section on "Green Topics": numerous articles, some of them fairly technical, on various aspects of building, renovating, and living in a green home, or working in a green building.

## Printing

Putting words onto paper has all sorts of environmental issues: logging forests, chemicals in the waste water, paper going into landfills after it's read, carbon impact of powering all those presses (to name a few).

However, you have lots of leeway to choose a printer who's working hard to minimize negative environmental impacts. Things to look for include

- ✓ Forest Stewardship Council or other reputable certification that monitors chain-of-custody from the time the wood is harvested until the paper is used (note: there are several different levels of FSC certification, so make sure you know what you're getting)

- ✓ Recycled paper, processed without chlorine bleach, with a high post-consumer waste (PCW) percentage

- ✓ Renewable energy used for all or most of the printing plant's energy needs (a net-zero building is even better)

- ✓ Short-run and on-demand printing options, allowing customers to use just-in-time inventory management instead of warehousing large quantities of printed materials.

- ✓ Recycling of paper-roll ends and other usable scrap

- ✓ Biodegradable, vegetable-based inks

- ✓ Zero contamination of water sources through waste discharge

Most printing companies offer at least a selection of recycled paper these days (and often at prices comparable to non-recycled). Some go much farther, incorporating many of the items in our checklist, above. And some actively market their green commitments; my eighth book, Guerrilla Marketing Goes Green, examines three different attempts by three different printers to make themselves attractive to green customers.

## Lodging

As with printing, pretty much every hotel, inn, and B&B has adopted at least some green best practices—if nothing else, the relatively recent custom of not changing all the towels and linens every day.

But in this industry, too, the smart ones are doing much more—such as:

- ✓ Installing water-conserving showerheads, toilets, and faucet aerators

- ✓ Serving filtered water in reusable pitchers and glasses, instead of water bottles and disposable cups

- ✓ Generating power through solar, wind, hydro, etc.

- ✓ Incorporating local organic food into meal and snack choices—and accommodating greener diets such as vegetarian and vegan

- ✓ Composting food wastes, either on-site or by donating to local farmers

- ✓ Putting plantings and potted plants in public areas

- ✓ Setting no-smoking policies

And they're basing much of their marketing on these initiatives. Here, for instance, is a passage from the home page of a very environmentally aware B&B: "first solar-powered, off-the-grid, bed and breakfast [in the state]. Our B&B opened in 2008 so we could showcase the ease of solar-living, provide you with a 'green' getaway, and share our land, our animals and our farm. We are just 5 minutes from town, but light years from the noise, hustle, and hassle of city life."

How can you incorporate more green principles into a conventional business—and how can you then get the most marketing advantage from doing so?

# d.light: Bringing Sustainable Lighting to Address Desperate Need

Perhaps you've read the game-shifting book The Fortune at the Bottom of the Pyramid, by C.K. Prahalad (you can read my review at www.principledprofit.com/subscribe-2#fortune). Arguing that the most economically disadvantaged people on the planet not only create a great market for those entrepreneurs brave enough to

 venture into that territory, but also that developing countries provide a terrific testing ground for innovation and cost control, Prahalad offers numerous examples of companies that are profiting handsomely while serving the poorest of the poor.

Here in the green world, we can look at that innovation potential through a lens of deep sustainability and multiple benefits. And the possibilities are awesome.

It's been a while since I've profiled a company in this space. This month, we take a look at one of those companies, simultaneously addressing poverty, education, air pollution/toxic fumes/health risks, energy savings, carbon footprint, and more—and making a huge difference in lives of those at the bottom of the economic pyramid. And the company does all this with a simple three-item product line.

d.light, headquartered in San Francisco and with additional offices in China, India, and Kenya, sells inexpensive freestanding bright-light LED lanterns with lifetime batteries powered by dual solar/plug-in electric chargers. The company's mission statement: "to create new freedoms for customers without access to reliable power so they can enjoy a brighter future."

And to accomplish this mission, the company employs a deeply holistic analysis of the problems faced by people at the bottom of the heap, and how a reliable and renewable source of good light can help solve them.

The lights go into two types of environments: places where light has been supplied by kerosene (or, conceivably, open fires)—and those with no pre-existing night-time light source.

If the lantern replaces an existing kerosene model, it accomplishes many desirable goals: providing a better quality of light that needs no fuel, does not produce toxic fumes, has no risk of setting the house on fire, reduces  pollution, and leaves considerably more money in the hands of the family using the lantern—because the savings over purchasing kerosene typically pays for the lantern in about two months.

Where the lantern provides light in a previously unlit area, the benefits are different, but just as significant: four more hours per day of productive time. Children can advance much farther with their studies; cottage industries, farms, and microbusinesses can produce and sell more. In short, the lamp becomes a ladder out of poverty.

Using classic Prahalad-inspired design principles, the units are cheap, extremely durable, and designed for multiple environments. A company video shows the lamps dropped from a high balcony and run over by a car, and still working afterward. At least one of the three models can be mounted on a wall or ceiling. The top-line model can also charge mobile phones. In developing countries, payment plans can be arranged for less than the previous cost of kerosene; in developed countries, 10 percent of the proceeds goes to fund lamps for children who could not buy them. Worldwide, they're sold with a two-year free-replacement warranty.

And the company, currently operating 6000 retail outlets in 40 countries, is very successful, both financially and in the social and environmental good it has created. As of February 28, 2013, the company claims:

- ✓ 13,638,438 "lives empowered" [that is, units sold]

- ✓ 3,409,610 school-aged children reached with solar lighting

- ✓ $275,817,462 saved in energy-related expenses

- ✓ 3,589,490,280 productive hours created for working and studying

- ✓ 656,952 tons of $CO_2$ offset

- ✓ 10,115,224 kWh generated from renewable energy source

(You can find the latest update of these statistics at www.dlightdesign.com/impact-dashboard/ ).

These stats, as I confirmed by e-mail discussion with company spokesperson Darin Kingston of the India office, were arrived at by looking at the maximum possible utilization for each category—and that means they may be overstating the benefits somewhat.

I asked Darin if he was double-counting—wasn't it true that if you max out the possible benefit, you can have either the $275 million in energy savings and the 657-ton $CO_2$ offset (replacing kerosene) OR the 3.6 billion newly productive hours (replacing darkness), but not both at once? But he assured me that no, they're not double-counting; the productivity benefit stems from the longer number of hours and better quality of light compared to kerosene. He did acknowledge that the stats assume a one-to-one relationship between the new lanterns and the kerosene lamps they replace.

Company executives hope to grow that user base from 13 million all the way to 100 million by the end of the decade—perhaps not an unrealistic estimate considering the company was only conceived of in 2004, following founder Sam Goldman's encounter as a Peace Corps volunteer in Africa with a neighbor child who had been badly burned in a kerosene spill.

It's good to see a company doing well by doing so much good—and combining environmental, social, and health benefits to serve the most needy.

# Nature's Business Model:
## 100 Percent Recycling, Zero Energy Consumption

Recycling, as we usually think of it, is a huge step forward compared to letting materials rot (or worse, not rot, ever) in a landfill. But recycling, the way it typically works, has its own issues. Conventional recycling requires massive inputs of energy to convert our trash into something not-quite-as-usable as the original material.

 So, for instance, high-quality petroleum-based PET is good enough to store beverages for human consumption. When mingled with other plastics and processed at a recycling plant, it's good enough to make "cloth" for shopping bags, or planks for decking and park benches. But it's no longer good enough to store things that people will drink.

Now the good news: the world gives us many better models than this. In biology, things work differently. Every biological element breaks up (I am deliberately not saying "breaks down") into an input for something else—starting with the basic lifecycle: animals convert oxygen into carbon dioxide, the breath-of-life for plants—and plants convert the $CO_2$ to our breath-of-life: oxygen. How cool is that?

Similarly, think of how compost works. A tree branch falls in the woods—or a family gathers their organic wastes in a bin outside.

Various insects, mammals, birds, and fungi begin to digest it. And eventually, miraculously, it turns into a brand new product: fresh, nutrient-rich soil.

And both the breath cycle and the compost cycle (among many other examples in nature) do their amazing work with zero waste, and with zero need for human-produced energy.

Humans can look at how nature works and come up with fresh, creative, dare-I-say brilliant new processes to do what nature does, and to do it without consuming energy. The trick is to look at what can use any particular waste product as a new input for a new process.

I've known about this for quite a few years, and have several examples of this thinking in my eighth book, Guerrilla Marketing Goes Green. Here, for instance, is an excerpt from the book, discussing the amazing work of an entrepreneur named John Todd:

In downtown Burlington and South Burlington, Vermont, you'll find a very unusual industrial park: a place where brewery wastes turn into a growing environment for mushrooms—and in the process create an enjoyable biopark, a green and vibrant ecosystem in the middle of the business district, where downtown workers can enjoy a unique natural setting.

Welcome to the Intervale, 700 acres of sustainable enterprises and ecofriendly public spaces.

Todd, like other visionaries I profile in the book, is an entrepreneur. He is making money leveraging nature's principles to remedy major issues such as pollution and rampant disease—both human-caused and nature caused. He's using biological principles to clean up stagnant lakes, to purify water in developing countries where safe water is a rarity.

Not that it's always simple. Listen to Todd explain what he did to clean up a lagoon that had been choking on the waste from a chicken processing plant:

"We planted restorers with 28,000 different species of higher plants and animals. It grew very quickly. Each was designed to break down or sequester different compounds. We reduced the electrical power to convert the waste by 80 percent and cut capital costs in half."

One of the underlying principles in this work is sharing resources among different pieces of the system and changing the paradigm about what's left over. Instead of disposing of a waste stream, Todd encourages people to think about how to use that material as an input. The goal is  zero emissions: no waste generation at all. If wastes are considered as inputs, they can lead to new commercial enterprises—for instance, a mushroom farm. All of a sudden, the cost of waste disposal turns into capital for a new revenue stream.

This is how the natural world works, at least when undisturbed by human pollution. When these systems are integrated together, they not only eliminate waste, but also provide shared synergy, reduce costs, spread technical and legal expertise, and create both economic and environmental improvements—as occurred at the Intervale, where biowastes feed a commercial fish farm that also cleans the water, and the waste heat from a wood-fired power plant is recaptured to heat the complex.

But the real lesson is this: every problem is an economic opportunity for a visionary entrepreneur. And those who can solve the world's problems with zero waste, high-quality outputs, and zero grid-based or human-produced energy are on track for success.

Will YOU be the next to create a business like this?

(Note: This article was inspired by the article, "A 'Circular Economy': Why the Next Packaging Will Be Grown, Not Manufactured," on Good: http://www.good.is/posts/mushrooms-based-packaging-and-designing-a-circular-economy

# Educate Your Customers to Do an Easy "**Green Reboot**"

As a business owner or manager, or as someone who works in a nonprofit or government agency, you probably have more influence than you think. Why not use that influence to both help your customers go green in ways they may not have thought about AND establish yourself even more firmly in their minds as a green organization that cares about the world. Forward-thinking companies around the world have been doing this for years—why not you?

Every point of interaction is a chance to educate your public: product packaging, in-store signage, advertisements, social media messaging, press coverage, a bulletin board in the reception area, the home page of your website and Facebook page, email and printed newsletters, brochures, and more—all opportunities to do good in the world by talking about the green steps you take, and the green steps your readers, viewers, listeners, and customers can take.

## What sorts of messages can you promote?

Of course, you want to discuss the green steps your organization has taken or will take shortly: the motivation for the change, the impact it has, the way it changes what is possible.

But why stop there? Use this "bully pulpit" to educate and inform a captive audience about why and how THEY should go green.

The how is as important as the why; lots of people are philosophically inclined to go green but have never really thought about the easy ways they can go greener in their personal lives.

And much of that lack is because of bad training—so you can make a difference by helping people retrain. It makes even better sense if you pick aspects of green behavior that relate directly to your own mission. Here are some examples:

We are trained to turn the faucet on full blast and leave it spewing precious water the whole time we wash a dish or brush our teeth. Educate your customers to turn on a small stream of water during the actual washing and rinsing, and to turn it completely off for the between part while they scrub or brush. Dentists, dish soap companies, sponge and kitchen appliance manufacturers or retailers: this is an opportunity for you. Run a restaurant? Post water-saving tips in your restroom or place them on a table tent.

We are trained to pull off a huge wad of toilet paper every time, most of which is completely wasted. Educate your customers at how effectively they can wipe with just a few squares—especially if you make or distribute paper products, or bathroom fixtures.

We are trained to fill up a whole kettle every time we want just one cup of tea, then to either pour the extra down the drain—behavior that borders on criminal, if you ask me—or waste energy to reboil the same water again, sometimes several times. Florists and garden supply stores, why not suggest that your customers water the plants with the surplus water, once it's cool? Plate and cutlery companies can recommend soaking dishes with the extra. Tea and energy companies can point out that the tea is better tasting if it's not reboiled, but in a way that discourages the down-the-drain "solution." Kettle makers can run contests for the best ways to recycle the extra water left in the kettle.

We are trained to jump in a car, by ourselves, and drive even very short distances. Ridesharing companies can encourage carpooling; bicycle and mass transit companies as well as healthcare providers can demonstrate the benefits of not driving at all.

Need more ideas about your opportunities to connect with your customers and change their behavior? Here in New England, there's a famous old slogan that can help you discover the possibilities: "Use it up, wear it out, make it do, or do without."

One resource that can help educate your customers is an e-book I've written called *Painless Green: 111 Tips to Help the Environment, Lower Your Carbon Footprint, Cut Your Budget, and Improve Your Quality of Life-With No Negative Impact on Your Lifestyle*. Contact me if you'd like to use this resource in your educational efforts.

# How is the **Green Economy Saving Money** in Your Business?

You often hear that going green is too expensive. Answer those critics with the ways going green is actually cheaper than staying brown. And there are many of those "low-hanging fruit" savings areas. So you can put those into place in your own business, start saving money to fund more expensive green improvements, and gain some bragging rights in your marketing.

What are we talking about? Here are two among dozens of possibilities.

## Switching to LEDs

Switching out any remaining incandescent light bulbs for LEDs (you can skip CFLs, which are not as efficient as LEDs and have waste disposal issues because they contain mercury). Using the savings calculator at

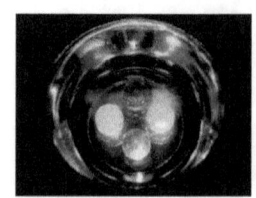

http://www.ledwaves.com/led-calc.html

shows just how much you can save. Let's say you run a retail store. If you replace 50 100-watt, 1000-hour lifespan bulbs that cost you $1 each with 10-watt, 50,000-hour bulbs that cost $10 each, over the life of the bulbs, you get to bank an extra $24,991.00—based on operating 10 hours a day at a relatively low commercial electricity rate of 10 cents per kilowatt hour. You break even less than three months after switching the bulbs.

Not bad—but now let's say you run a high-ceilinged location like a basketball court. You replace the same 50 bulbs, but you also have to pay a worker to go out in a cherry picker every time you change a bulb. How much does the labor, fuel, and depreciation/maintenance cost you? $50? $100? More? Let's be generous to the nongreens and say it's $50, and furthermore, we'll say your worker replaces an average of three bulbs every time, rather than just one, so the net cost per bulb is $16.70 for the labor and vehicle use, plus another buck for the replacement incandescent bulb. Thus each new incandescent bulb is going to cost $17.70 to purchase and install.

The calculator informs us that you eliminated 2500 bulb changes by switching to LEDs, and you won't have to change them again for 13 years. If I'm figuring this correctly, multiplying $17.70 times 2500 saves an astonishing $4,425,000.

## Changing Your Printing and Copying Habits

Here's an example more relevant to smaller entrepreneurs, including home-based businesses like my own. Six years ago, when my laser printer wore out, I replaced it with a duplexing printer— one that's designed to print on both sides. I also  changed my default setting to duplex printing (Note: I don't advise feeding used paper back into a single-sided printer; you might encounter problems like toner getting sucked into the rollers.)

Just this simple change dropped my paper bill by about 40 percent (not 50 percent, because some print jobs are an odd number of pages). The savings added up quickly because I use recycled paper that costs about $40 or $50 per case.

I also bumped up the font size for screen viewing—another simple change that saved oodles of paper. I used to print documents as short as five pages because it was fatiguing to read them onscreen. But by setting the View mode to 125 or 150 percent, I can usually read 20 or 25 pages comfortably.

And I got in the habit of using Print Preview. Often, especially when printing from the Web, I see that I don't need to print several pages at the end. In Word documents, I often find a single blank page at the end, and delete before printing.

In short, by thinking strategically about printing, you can lower your costs and your carbon footprint. Similarly, before copying, think about who really needs to see the document, and whether it makes more sense to send it electronically rather than run off a bunch of copies.

I'd love to hear what you're doing to save money while greening your own business. Please write to me at shel AT greenandprofitable.com with the subject line, "How I'm Greening My Business Affordably" (you might even get publicity in a future column).

# Biofuels: **Good and Bad** Models to **Learn From**

Those of us who want a greener world can learn a lot from the biofuel industry. Both positive and negative lessons abound.

The first and perhaps most important lesson is to think things through. What appears on the surface to be a wonderful solution may not be so wonderful after all. In the case of biofuels, a lot of the technologies turned out to be full of unintended consequences.

Two technologies have been particularly troubling: corn ethanol and burning biomass. Both have turned out to be expensive, polluting, high-carbon-footprint, and resource-consuming. And both have diverted both land and what grows on the land from their highest potential uses.

Corn ethanol takes prime farmland out of food production and diverts it to energy. Wood-burning biomass plants lead to forest destruction. Neither is clean, and with corn ethanol, the ratio of energy consumed to energy generated is far from pretty. Both worsen the potential for harmful climate change, and both can lead to problems including monocropping, drastically reduced biodiversity and wildlife habit, and even higher food prices.

But should we write off biofuels altogether?
Not at all.

Many much more promising technologies can actually reduce pollution and generate energy without interfering with food production or habitat. For instance:

The farm I live on is currently installing a methane digester that will actually remove greenhouse gasses while providing enough electricity to power 250 homes. Its inputs? Cow manure and food waste!

In Brazil, sugarcane waste underpins a vast ethanol industry, strengthened by a government requirement to mix ethanol with gasoline (and government incentives to produce ethanol), all the way back to 1976. As a result, almost the entire Brazilian vehicle fleet runs either on flex-fuel mixtures of ethanol and gasoline, or on pure ethanol.
(More information: en.wikipedia.org/wiki/Ethanol_fuel_in_Brazil)

In the United States, where I live, many companies are successfully harvesting waste frying oil from fast-food restaurants and converting the waste oil to biodiesel. One particularly spiffy model is Green Circle North Carolina, which adds some beautiful new pieces to create a circle of community self-sufficiency: donating a portion of the profits to the schools, offering restaurants the PR benefits of supporting local school districts, and then selling the biodiesel to those school districts to power their school buses. When we as green entrepreneurs create these sorts of win-win-win programs, the whole world benefits.

There have also been many successful experiments generating ethanol with nonfood crops that can grow on marginal land, such as switchgrass. These have tended to yield more energy and create fewer greenhouse gases.

(More information: www.scientificamerican.com/article.cfm?id=grass-makes-better-ethanol-than-corn). And then there's the so-called Q Microbe, that its backers claim will digest far more cellulose and produce much more energy from the same amount of biomass. However, commercializing the Q Microbe, first identified by researchers at the University of Massachusetts several years ago, has been off to a very rocky start. Qteros (the company that has tried to bring this technology to market) has faced many funding and operational challenges—including changes in ownership and having to close its plant—and its future is unclear.

From my perspective, the more successful and promising technologies have something in common: they create energy out of what we're accustomed to thinking of as waste: materials that would have either  clogged up landfills or emitted greenhouse gases when incinerated. Furthermore, they are not the food parts of food crops; they're either waste parts of food plants, or plants that are not used for food (and aren't grown on prime agricultural land).

In other words, they are part of a holistic approach to thinking about the integration of our energy and food systems, and not a poorly-thought-out kludge grafted onto a system not designed to accommodate it, all too often with disastrous consequences.

In one sense, biofuel is our oldest energy source. When aboriginal societies first discovered, thousands of years ago, that fire could not only keep them warm on cold winter nights but could preserve food while making it both easier to digest and better tasting, they were burning wood and plant matter. Back then, of course, they didn't worry about greenhouse gas emissions.

In short, as with wind, solar, and hydro, we can find both right and wrong ways to develop new energy sources. In tomorrow's world, sensible biofuel will be part of the mix.

# What I **Learned** from my **Energy Audit**

January was much colder than usual here—and my old farmhouse (built in 1743) was feeling unusually chilly—especially the kitchen, which we'd just redone.

It had been a few years since our last energy audit, so I set one up.

The first thing I learned was why my house has felt so much colder this year. The house had been insulated by the previous owner, probably in the 1970s. And the insulation was fiberglass, which has a definite lifespan. We'd been told the last time we'd had an audit that the insulation was aging; this time, we were told it was past its usefulness.

But beyond the worn-out fiberglass (not the most ecological material to begin with)—the whole house was leaking air all over the place. As I walked around the house with the auditor, he pointed out chinks in the basement foundation, spaces between beams and walls, beams and ceilings, and walls and ceilings, gaps between the wooden pieces of our skylights.

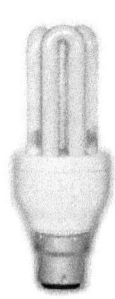

And we finally found out why the kitchen was even colder than the rest of the house: our new energy-saving LED light fixtures, ironically enough, were not insulated and tapped into the very coldest part of the house: a second-floor kneewall running the length of the longest side. The quality of light and the amazingly low energy consumption of the lights is fabulous—but who knew it would have such an impact on our home heating?

No wonder we've had to turn the thermostat higher lately!

The auditor suggested we could fix the LED air infiltration problem with spray-foam insulation. However, in that room, where we just spent a large amount of money to redo it, aesthetics are a big consideration. When I applied some of that foam in another part of the house, I found it very hard to control, and the results were less-than-pretty. So I think we'll wait until we can find someone to do it who can make it look nice.

The vendor for the energy audit outlined several steps we could do to alleviate the situation—each of which cost about double what I would have expected to pay. If we did everything he told us to, we'd have been looking at well over $18,000. Even if it saved us as much as $500 per year—highly unlikely, considering that's about 25 percent of an entire heating bill—that's a 36-year payback. Not a very good return on investment, even for a green guy like me.

Fortunately, since he had walked me around the house and shown me the areas where cold air was infiltrating, I could fix the most glaring problems myself, with rope caulk or spray-foam insulation. I am doing this a little at a time, and already notice huge improvement in the room where I've been concentrating: my grown daughter's former bedroom, which is where I keep my exercise bike. Just by caulking the skylight and foaming some of the air spaces, I'm able to use a lot less electric heat in that room. It doesn't get nearly as cold, and when I preheat the room before an exercise session, I can come back in a lot faster. In short, the savings are immediate.

Over the next few weeks, I'll be sealing up a lot of these cracks all around the house. I'm expecting a substantial reduction of energy use and much greater comfort as I work my way through the project. Cost? About $20 US, and some short periods of time when I need a break from the computer anyway.

Also fortunately, we live in an area where many vendors are competing in the insulation arena. So we'll get a few more estimates, and find a vendor who can deliver value as well as comfort.

## Lessons and Takeaways

So what did we learn from this experience?

- ✓ Even a building that was well-insulated in its day may need some refreshing after some years.

- ✓ Look at value received over money spent. Do the little, inexpensive things ithat have a big impact to get a measurable result.

- ✓ Don't accept the first estimate you receive; check a few competitors.

Postscript: We had a different vendor come in to do an energy audit a few months later, through our utility company. Because the utility is under pressure to reduce demand, it actually funds not only the audit, but much of the work. During the audit, nearly all our remaining non-LED light bulbs, our showerheads, our thermostat, and a couple of our power strips were all replaced at no cost to us. Following the audit, we contracted with the firm to implement most of the recommendations.

The end result: for a few hundred dollars out of pocket, we got extensive insulation and a much warmer, more comfortable house with a far lower fuel consumption—and even counting the utility's contribution, a total cost of about 1/9 the first vendor's estimate.

* * *

I enjoyed writing this column from 2010 to 2014, and I think I provided very high value for those who read it. Unfortunately, I never got enough markets to make the project economically viable.

As I move in the direction of helping companies see the value in solving problems like hunger, poverty, war, and climate catastrophe, I can no longer afford the luxury of doing this column for the few markets that subscribed. So this will be the last issue for a while.

I'd love to bring it back, if I can get to a minimum number of subscribers each paying just $10 per month. If you have possible markets for me, please drop me a line at shel AT greenandprofitable.com with the subject "Column Market."

Disclaimer: The very observant among you may notice that some examples come up more than once. Keep in mind that this ebook is a compilation of a monthly column that ran for four years. I have organized the columns by topic rather than chronologically here, and as a result, columns that may have been years apart end up close to each other in the same ebook. Yes, some examples are repeated, but they were inserted to make different points, at different times. Please also note that nothing in this ebook series should be taken as legal or professional advice, and as in any situation, your results may vary as you implement the tips and ideas.

# About Shel Horowitz and
## Business For a Better World

Green business profitability expert Shel Horowitz shows businesses how to profit both by going green and by addressing problems like hunger and poverty, war, violence, and catastrophic climate change. Active in both marketing and the environment since his teen years in the early 1970s, Shel is the award-winning author of eight books including long-running Amazon category bestseller *Guerrilla Marketing Goes Green*.

- ✓ As a consultant, Shel brings laser focus to turning problems into opportunities, opening new markets, and helping you identify potential partners.

- ✓ As a marketing and informational copywriter trained in journalism, Shel is known for his clear writing, ability to make technical concepts accessible, and his skill in telling "the story behind the story" to move people to action.

- ✓ As an international speaker and trainer, Shel combines dynamic vocal style with powerful graphics and gets his audiences actively involved. He's spoken at major business and environmental conferences in locations as diverse as Istanbul, Davos (Switzerland), and Honolulu.

After over a decade actively assisting green businesses with their marketing, Shel branched out in 2014 to help businesses seize profit opportunities in turning hunger and poverty into sufficiency, war and violence into peace, and catastrophic climate change into planetary balance—and helping individuals reclaim their power to actively create this better world.

Shel is happy to talk to you about helping in any of these areas. Reach him at 413-586-2388 (8 a.m. to 10 p.m. US Eastern Time), email shel AT greenandprofitable.com,or find him on Twitter @ShelHorowitz.

Shel also has a gift for you: a free copy of his ebook, *Painless Green: 111 Tips to Help the Environment, Lower Your Carbon Footprint, Cut Your Budget, and Improve Your Quality of Life—With No Negative Impact on Your Lifestyle*. To claim your free copy of this $9.95 ebook, visit PainlessGreenBook.com/earthday and use the code, G&Pebook.

One more set of gifts, FREE with your no-cost subscription to Shel Horowitz's monthly Clean and Green Newsletter:

- ✓ Seven Tips to Gain Marketing Traction as a Green Guerrilla

- ✓ Seven Weeks to a Greener Business: once a week for seven weeks, tips on going greener with printing, energy saving, waste reduction, water conservation, transportation, going deep-green, and of course, green marketing.

- ✓ Plus the informative monthly newsletter, published since 1997 and featuring a business tip or profile plus a book review each issue.

**Sign up in the upper-right-hand corner at** http://greenandprofitable.com.

www.ingramcontent.com/pod-product-compliance
Lightning Source LLC
Chambersburg PA
CBHW070932180526
45168CB00003B/1041